LET'S HAVE A MILKY WAY JOURNEY

DR. JAGADEESH PILLAI

Made with ♥ on the Notion Press Platform
www.notionpress.com

Dedicated to those who want to learn about the Milky Way Galaxy in a brief and concise way.

Contents

Contents

Preface

The Milky Way Galaxy is an awe-inspiring entity, with its majestic spiral arms filled with celestial bodies in all directions. It is estimated to contain more than 200 billion stars, plus gas and dust particles, swirling around a supermassive black hole at its center. Our own sun is located on one of the minor spiral arms near the outer edge of the galaxy, making our view of the Milky Way's structure incomplete as we can only observe about 0.000002 percent of it. Despite this limitation however, astronomers have used a variety of powerful telescopes and instruments to map out nearly two thirds of the galaxy's structure enabling humanity to understand a little bit more about our home among the stars.

Everyone is eager to learn more about the Milky Way galaxy. I have compiled my notes and findings while researching this fascinating celestial body.

Prayer

Ganga tharanga ramaneeya jata kalapam,
Gowri niranthara vibhooshitha vama bhagam,
Narayana priya mananga madapaharam,
Varanasi pura pathim Bhajha Viswanatham ||

About The Author

Dr. Jagadeesh Pillai four times Guinness World Record holder, a voracious reader, writer, and true research scholar was born in Varanasi, the abode of Lord Shiva. He is Ph.D. in Vedic Science. He is a multi-faceted polymath with innate qualities, creative ideas and many remarkable achievements. Although his roots extend back to "Gods own Country"(Kerala), the residents of Varanasi feel proud of him and adore him as a child of Varanasi who caters to every individual in need without any expectations. A deep study into his profile reflects that he has added so many feathers to his cap which makes him quite unique. He is a four times Guinness Book of World Records Holder in the following subjects :

1. "Script to Screen" which he achieved by producing and directing a state of art animation film within the shortest time possible by breaking the earlier set record by Canadians. There are many national and international Awards and Recognitions to his credit.

2. Longest Line of Post Cards which he has done on the occasion of 163 years of Indian Postal Day by 16300 post cards. The event was also connected with a questionnaire about Indian Flag.

3. Largest Poster Awareness Campaign – This was achieved by designing an awareness campaign on the subject "Beti Bachao – Beti Padhao".

4. Largest Envelop – Towards tribute to Prime Minister's

initiative 'Make in India' – he has created about 4000 sq meter envelop using waste papers.

5. Attempted by lighting 70000 candles on a 210 kg cake to celebrate the 70th Indian Independence day recorded in World Records India.

6. Attempted a documentary on Dhamek Stupa of Sarnath dubbing in 17 languages, result is waiting from Guinness World Records.

He is versatile in Gita teaching. The young generation is fond of his Gita teaching and he has changed the life of many young through his continued motivational boost up and teachings.

He has composed and sung Gayatri Mantra in 1000 different tunes.

He has composed and sung Hanuman Chalisa in 108 different tunes.

He has composed and sung hundreds of Sanskrit Bhajans, Patriotic songs, etc.

He has written and directed so many short films and documentaries for awareness campaigns.

He has done voluntary services to UP Police and Kerala Police to spread awareness campaigns on the various issue through videos and photography.

He is on the path of authoring thousands of books on Indian culture, Indian Temples, and the life of extraordinary people.

It is hard to believe that he has produced and directed more than 100 Documentaries on a particular city (Varanasi) which is done by a single person.

He has helped and guided more than 25 boys and girls to achieve world records through various creative and innovative methods.

A multifaceted person who can apply the best of his intellect using the God-given blessings which have been showered upon every human being granting them an immense capacity to learn, experience, and experiment with many things and do wonders in this world of discrimination and disparities.

He is a teacher and a student at the same time who always learns every day and teaches every day. As a master, his weakness was that he never sticks to a particular subject. Perhaps this weakness gives him the strength to master any area which he came across.

Each of his days dawned with learning a new topic and he spend most of his time experimenting and researching it.

He is also a selfless social activist and a motivational speaker.

His life was full of struggle, ups and downs, and failures.

But he never gave up and faced all his trials and tribulations full of confidence. Today he is a successful young man with a lot of enthusiasm and rich life experience.

He has sung full Ram Charita Manas 151 hours audio by his own composition. He has also sung the whole Bhagavad-Gita in his own composition with a rhythmic background.

He has also sung “Lokah Samastha Sukhino Bhavantu” in 50 different languages.

Currently working on a detailed and scientific study on Veda, Upanishad, Puranas, Bhagavad Gita, etc.

He has composed and sung Hanuman Chalisa in 108 different compositions and Gayatri Mantra in 1008 different compositions.

Awards

Four Times Guinness World Records

Winner of Mahatma Gandhi Vishwa Shanti Puraskar

Mahatma Gandhi Global Peace Ambassador

Kashi Ratna Award

Dr. APJ Abdul Kalam Motivational Person of the Year 2017

Mother Teresa Award

Indira Gandhi Priyadarshini Award

Bharat Vikas Ratna Award

Udyog Ratna Award

Vigyan Prasar Award

Poorvanchal Ratn Samman

CHAPTER ONE

THE MILKY WAY GALAXY

The Milky Way is the home of our solar system and its planets. Appearing as a hazy band of light that extends across the night sky, its origins stretch further back than recorded history. To understand its appearance from Earth, we must consider a range of factors.

The Milky Way is a barred spiral galaxy, estimated to contain around 100 billion stars, with our Sun making up just one of them. This galactic structure creates a characteristic arms pattern of stars when viewed from above. From the Earth, this arms pattern occupies a flattened arc of stars, visible at all longitudes of the sky.

Beyond that, the Milky Way is dim, with our view further impaired by light pollution from cities and the moon. The faintness of the Milky Way is compounded by its gaseous component, blocked from view by dust clouds that form up in Earth's atmosphere. When the night sky has clear conditions, the Milky Way is best viewed from a dark location away from artificial light in the direction of the galactic centre, typically between Sagittarius and Scorpio.

This characteristically grey-white band of stars consists of five regions of varying clarity, based on the number of stars within them and our viewing angle. From the most clearly visible to the faintest it is; the S-shaped Milky Way's state which is easily seen near the galactic centre of Sagittarius, the unilluminated dark patch that encompasses the galaxy, moving further out along the arms the band of the Milky Way, followed by the halo, a pervasive faint band of stars, and finally the outer limits of the Milky Way in the night sky.

The Milky Way is a constantly expanding galactic phenomenon, and astrological knowledge allows us to identify certain festivals and events with the alignment of certain stars and constellations. From the Earth to the heavens, the Milky Way has provided awe-inspiring views throughout human history and remains a source of fascination and wonder.

CHAPTER TWO

MORE MILKY WAY GALAXIES

The Milky Way is one of the most massive galaxies in the observable universe. With a diameter of around 120,000 light-years, it contains more than 200 billion stars and an unimaginably large number of planets, star systems, nebulae, and other cosmic structures. It is the home galaxy for our own solar system and many other star systems, including the giant stars, the largest known gas clouds, and entire star clusters.

The Milky Way contains many different kinds of galaxies, with both spiral and elliptical shapes. The majority of the Milky Way is composed of spiral galaxies, with a smaller fraction being elliptical galaxies. Spiral galaxies contain more stars and star clusters, with a more dynamic, varied mix of gas and dust. Elliptical galaxies are generally more static, containing less gas and dust and smaller numbers of stars and star clusters.

The Milky Way is a barred spiral galaxy, which means that its arms follow a pattern around its central bar-like region. This gives the Milky Way its classic "teapot" shape, though the arms of the galaxy can become distorted by the gravitational pull of nearby galaxies. The barred shape also allows it to be distinguished from other types of spiral galaxies.

The Milky Way is part of the so-called "Local Group" of galaxies, which includes the Andromeda Galaxy, the Large and Small Magellanic Clouds, and several other smaller galaxies. The Milky Way is the second-largest member of this group, after the Andromeda Galaxy. Beyond the Local Group lies the "Virgo Supercluster", which contains hundreds of large and small galaxies, many of which appear to be connected to our own.

The exact number of Milky Way galaxies is difficult to

determine, as they can be obscured by dust, gas and other space debris. Astronomers estimate that the number of Milky Way galaxies is somewhere between 170 and 200 billion galaxies. Some of these galaxies may be much larger or smaller than our own, but the combination of stars, gas, dust, and other cosmic material makes the Milky Way an incredibly unique, diverse and vast celestial structure.

The Milky Way is one of the most beautiful, awe-inspiring and mysterious galaxies in the universe. Its vast expanse of stars and star clusters, its bright and colourful nebulae, its mysterious voids, and its intricate structures offer an inexhaustible universe of exploration and discovery. We may never know the full extent of its wonders, but its existence is far more fascinating than any number of words could ever describe.

CHAPTER THREE

ALIVE AND MOVING GALAXY

The universe is a place of wonder and awe. It contains wonders we scarcely comprehend and many mysteries remain unsolved. But if we take a deeper look into this great unknown, we can see that the disc of the galaxy is alive and moving.

To begin, it is important to point out the basic structure of the Milky Way galaxy referred to as the galactic disc. The disc contains the large Sprial arms with smaller central bar and bulge. As we peer into the galactic disc we can see that the process of galactic disc movement is continuous and turbulent on large scales. This happens because of a process called “ram pressure”. This is the push and pull of the stars and gas particles within the disc as they move around and interact with other stars or gases.

This process can cause stars to be accelerated to orbital velocities as fast as 200 km per second. Accelerations of this magnitude cause a star to move around the galactic disc in a periodic fashion, generating turbulence. Turbulence is caused when vast numbers of stars interact with each other or have other stars or gasses passing close by. The turbulence then causes stars to be deflected from their original orbits and accelerations, which further adds to the process of ‘ram pressure’ and movement within the disc.

In addition to the interstellar medium, supernovae also play a profound role in the motion of the galactic disc. Supernovae are the energetic explosions at the ends of stellar progression and occur when the star’s supply of fuel matter is used up. This process of stellar death can provide a boost to local gravities of stars and gas close by, causing them an increased velocity of motion. This in turn causes a large push and pull within the galactic disc which can accelerate many stars and send them into ever-evolving and turbulent movements.

Overall, the disc of the galaxy is seen to be alive with movements of stars and gases, caused by both the interstellar medium and supernovae. As stars orbits and move in a periodic fashion, ram pressure causes stars to be pushed and pulled around the disc in a turbulent almost chaotic manner, causing variation in motion speeds and trajectories as they interact with one another. It is this movement of the galactic disc that helps to form galaxies and keeps them constantly changing and evolving, providing us with an ever-changing canvas of our Milky Way galaxy.

CHAPTER FOUR

GALAXY CLOSET TO EARTH

The Milky Way is an enormous rotating disk-shaped spiral galaxy, which our Earth and all other known stars in our Solar System call home. As one of the closest galaxies to Earth, it is estimated to be about one hundred thousand parsecs (or about three hundred thousand light years) in diameter—quite vast.

The Milky Way is made up of many stars, gas, and dust, and is estimated to contain between two and four hundred billion stars. As a result, it is one of the largest and most massive galaxies in the observable universe. Additionally, its mass is estimated to approximately one trillion solar masses, which is equivalent to the mass of the sun multiplied by one trillion. This provides evidence of just how large and unobservable the Milky Way truly is.

The closest galaxy to Earth is the Andromeda Galaxy, also known as Messier 31 or M31. It is a lenticular galaxy approximately two and a half million light-years away and is the nearest major galaxy to us. M31 is estimated to be one hundred twenty thousand light-years across at its widest and is composed of about a trillion stars. It is visible to the naked eye from the Northern Hemisphere and is part of the Local Group, a gathering of 54 galaxies that includes the Milky Way, M31, and two other large spiral galaxies.

The Milky Way and the Andromeda Galaxy are two of the largest galaxies in the Local Group. Due to their relative proximity in the universe, M31 and our Milky Way are considered to interact, even though their two rotation planes are different and no direct collision has been observed yet. It is believed, however, that this interaction will result in a future galactic collision, which is expected to occur in approximately four billion years.

In summary, the closest galaxy to Earth is the Andromeda Galaxy, also known as M31 or Messier 31. It is part of the Local Group of 54 galaxies, containing a trillion stars, and is approximately two and a half million light-years away from us. Additionally, the Milky Way is the galaxy our

Earth and all other known stars in our Solar System call home and is estimated to be around one hundred thousand parsecs or three hundred thousand light years in diameter with a mass of approximately one trillion solar masses. Despite their differences, the Milky Way and Andromeda Galaxy are believed to interact, which could lead to a future galactic collision in about four billion years.

CHAPTER FIVE

GAIA REVELATIONS ABOUT THE MILKY WAY

Gaia, the European Space Agency's revolutionary mission, has been studying and mapping our Milky Way galaxy for the past three years since its launch in 2013. During that time it has made some amazing discoveries about this ever-changing region of space and provided us with a deep understanding of the Milky Way's many features and the stars that make it up. Here are five of the most fascinating revelations that Gaia has made about the Milky Way.

First, Gaia has revealed a vast number of stars within the Milky Way, nearly two times higher than what we originally thought. A whopping 1.7 billion stars were identified, precision-measured, and mapped out by the telescope, all of which were used to create, what some have called, the most detailed map of our galaxy ever.

Second, the map created by Gaia gave us a clearer picture of how our galactic disk orbits the center, allowing for better understanding of our galaxy's structure and motion. The map also showed the presence of a stellar halo, a group of stars located beyond the Milky Way's star-filled disk, which is believed to be the leftover material from an ancient merger between our galaxy and a smaller one.

Third, it was revealed that the Milky Way's stars are not evenly distributed, in both location and age. While some areas are filled with mostly young stars, other regions are completely devoid of any new stars, having instead much older ones. This is due to past galactic collisions with other galaxies and star clusters, which may have had an impact on the Milky Way's distribution of stars.

Fourth, a large number of stars have been defined as supergiants, or stars with a very high brightness relative to the average stars in the Milky Way. These supergiants can be seen even from Earth and are believed to have had an important role in our galaxy's history, as well as an ongoing influence on our galaxy's structure.

Finally, Gaia has given us an unprecedented look at the Milky Way's globular clusters. These are densely packed spherical collections of stars, which are thought to be very ancient and has remained unchanged in structure for billions of years. Gaia's findings on these clusters allowed us to further uncover their chemical composition, the dynamics of the clusters, and their origin.

Thanks to the incredible work of Gaia, we have gained more knowledge about our very own Milky Way than ever before. It has revealed an abundance of details on our galaxy's stellar population, structure, and formation that were previously unknown to us. Now that we know more of these fascinating insights, we can use the insights gained to further increase our understanding of the Milky Way and potentially unlock even more mysteries.

CHAPTER SIX

MYTH ABOUT MILKY WAY

The Milky Way is a majestic band of stars, visible in the night sky as a hazy strip across the heavens. The popular name has been used for a long time, probably giving rise to its myth.

Many cultures around the world have tried to explain the origin of the Milky Way. The ancient Romans, Greeks and Egyptians all have their own versions of mythology. The most popular myth is that the Milky Way is composed of drops of milk spilled by a goddess, usually Hera or Hera-Demeter. In Greek mythology, according to the mythographer Apollodorus, Zeus was nursing Heracles, his illegitimate son, and to preserve his anonymity, he released his milk across the sky. Another version of the myth claims that when Hera saw Heracles, who was being nourished with Zeus's milk, she became angry and spilled her own milk out of jealousy. This milk made a milky white "River of Heaven."

In Roman mythology, the Milky Way was known as Via Lactea, which means the Milky Way. It was said to have been the milk spilled from the goddess Juno when she was nursing the infant Hercules. The ancient Egyptians associated the Milky Way with the goddess Isis, who in her devotion to her son Horus, let her milk spill into the night sky. Native American cultures have a similar myth, believing the Milky Way is created when a supernatural figure weeps celestial tears.

The term "Milky Way" itself is derived from the Latin Via Lactea, which in turn comes from the Greek galaxias kuklos. This term means the 'White Circle' or 'Milky Way'. The name was officially adopted in Europe by the astronomer Johannes Kepler in the 1600s.

Most of the folklore and mythology associated with the name 'Milky Way' is just that - folklore and myth. Nevertheless, these stories are interesting, and remain a testament to the massive impact that the Milky Way has had on the human imagination for several centuries.

CHAPTER SEVEN

APPEARANCE OF MILKY WAY GALAXY

The Milky Way is a colossal gravitational structure that dominates the celestial sky. It is a beautiful spiral galaxy, estimated to be around 100,000 – 120,000 light-years in diameter, containing roughly an estimated 200 – 400 billion stars. From Earth, it appears as an immense white band of light arching across the night sky, stretching from one horizon to the other. It can also be seen in its entirety from certain places in the southern hemisphere, where the night sky is particularly dark.

The Milky Way is composed of four main components, which contain most of its stars, dust, and gas: a galactic disk, which forms the spiral shape, a bulge in the centre, a prominent bar shape, which can often be seen especially in long exposures, and a surrounding halo filled with gas and dark matter. From our perspective on Earth, it appears as a big, bright band of white arching across the sky. Although it appears to be thick and consistent, the Milky Way is actually composed of billions of stars, clouds of interstellar gas and dust, as well as large amounts of dark matter.

The Milky Way is believed to have formed around twelve billion years ago, when gigantic clouds of hydrogen and hydrogen-rich gas formed within the the interstellar medium. Over billions of years, the gas clouds slowly began to collapse under their own gravity, slowly forming denser fragmentations until the stars began to form from the denser molecular clouds of gas. By around thirteen billion years ago, the first proto-stars, the precursors to the stars that would make up the Milky Way, had ignited and began to form within the dense gas clouds. As these stars accumulated, the Milky Way began to grow, slowly acquiring more stars, dust, and gas over trillions of years, until it became the beautiful spiral structure we see today.

The Milky Way is composed of two major arms, the Sagittarius Arm and the Perseus Arm, with the solar system located within the Orion arm at the outer edge of the Milky Way, at around 28,000 light-years away from the galactic centre. The two major arms, as well as a number of smaller spiral arms, divide the Milky Way into distinct sections.

When viewed in long exposure photos, or with powerful optics, the Milky Way reveals its full beauty. The stars appear to be clustered together like adiamonds scattered against a background of black velvet. The stars form intricate patterns, such as the larger star clouds known as Messier Objects, and these patterns can reveal much about the structure of the Milky Way. The dust clouds illuminated by the stars, known as nebulae, appear as bright clouds of red, blue, and green. Star clusters, containing hundreds or even thousands of stars in a very small region, can be seen in the zigzagging arms of the Milky Way, like a myriad of miniature firework explosions.

CHAPTER EIGHT

MILKY WAY GALAXY AND THE EARTH

Earth is a pale blue dot, situated within the Milky Way Galaxy, an immense collection of stars, planets, and other matter that stretches across an estimated 100,000 to 180,000 light-years in diameter. Understanding how Earth fits within its galactic home requires vastly increased perspectives of distance and time.

Earth could be considered the center of the Milky Way, if one were to look at its night sky from a distant observer's point of view. Our planet is situated at a distance of 27,000 to 28,000 light-years from the galactic center. Yet, it is situated on the outer region of the Milky Way's arms.

Earth's galactic home is much more diverse than most people realize. It is an incredibly grand spiral system, with a central bulge, four main arms, and numerous smaller arms. Its core consists of an old and densely packed star cluster that is home to a supermassive black hole. Evidence suggests that the Milky Way is growing more rapidly in its centers due to star formation there.

The Milky Way is not a featureless plane of stars, however. It has many interesting features like nebulae- large clouds of dust and gas-, H II regions- bright areas of hot, ionized gas -, open clusters- small groups of relatively young stars- and young-stellar objects or YSOs- high-mass star complexes that are in the process of formation.

The Milky Way can also be broken down into the halo, the disk, and the bulge. The halo is a spherical region located outside the disk, where old stars and globular clusters can be found. The disk is flattened and situated in the center of the galaxy and is home to Earth and other young stars. The bulge contains both old and young stars and is located in the center of the Milky Way.

When viewed from far outside the galaxy, our home is indeed a breathtaking sight. Its sheer size and complexity create a profound admixture of darkness, light, and infinite stars. But Earth is just one small fraction of the Milky Way's bigger picture. Though our home, the Solar System and Earth, is situated in the outer region of one of its main arms, the Milky Way is composed of countless other stars, planets, and living things. It is this complexity, and the knowledge that we are only a microscopic dot within its grand scheme, that illuminates out awareness of place and purpose.

CHAPTER NINE

HOW MANY MILKY WAY GALAXIES ARE THERE

The universe is an unimaginably immense expanse of space, filled with an almost immeasurable number of galaxies. Our own stellar neighborhood, the Milky Way, is just one of these, and one of the closest to us. But how many other Milky Way-esque galaxies are out there? Although they are incredibly difficult to count, astronomers believe that the number of Milky Way-type galaxies, or spiral galaxies, in the universe is in the tens of billions, and possibly even higher.

The Milky Way itself has roughly 200 billion stars, and the universe is estimated to contain up to 10 trillion galaxies. The Milky Way is part of the Local Group of galaxies, which includes at least 34 other galaxies of various sizes, shapes, and types. It is estimated that 10 to 50 percent of galaxies in the Local Group are of the same type as the Milky Way. This gives us some indication of the sheer number of similar galaxies that must exist in the universe.

Spiral galaxies, like the Milky Way, form a distinct shape that has a bright bulge in the middle, then spiral arms that contain dust, gas, and stars. They are some of the brightest galaxies, largely due to the fact that they contain multiple star forming regions and many types of emission nebulae. The light from these so-called 'starburst galaxies' effectively outshines the rest of the cosmos.

Spiral galaxies are believed to form when pieces of gas and other materials become bound together by gravity in the primordial universe. As these materials smash together, they form rotating clouds of gas, dust, and stars that spiral outwards. Developing stars in these galaxies then ignite and emit the types of light we observe today. Spiral galaxies can be classified into four main types, based on the nature of their spiral arms. These various types include grand design spirals, flocculent spirals, intermediate spirals, and multiple-armed spirals.

In terms of the exact number of Milky Way-type galaxies in the universe, we still don't know for sure. The number could be in the hundreds of billions or even approaching one trillion, depending on the type and size of the galaxies studied. Some calculations suggest that the number could even be in the range of five trillion individual galaxies, though this is currently just a guess.

The Milky Way and other spiral galaxies are both captivating and awe-inspiring. Upon reflection, it can be truly mind-boggling to understand that in the vast expanse of the universe, one can find an unimaginably high number of similar galaxies – from the microscopic to the grandiose.

CHAPTER TEN

MILKY WAY GALAXY FOR CHILDREN

The Milky Way galaxy is an incredibly vast and complex astronomical entity, but it can surprisingly be easily explained to children aged ten and under using analogies, visuals, and stories. To begin, it's important to make sure that a basic understanding of the basic concepts of space is established. Explain the idea of stars, planets, and the sky in ways that a child can understand.

Once the basics of space have been established, explain to the child that the Milky Way is a type of galaxy. A galaxy is a vast collection of stars and other entities that is held together by gravity. Describe it to the child as if they were looking down on a group of stars that form together in a special shape, like a swirl or a circle. Describe the stars and planets as if they were all connected with strings, like a web. Give them a visual reference like a picture of a galaxy and point out the stars, planets, and dust that make up the Milky Way.

After the child has been introduced to the concept of the Milky Way, explain its importance in the universe. The Milky Way is a massive disc-shaped formation held together by gravity and made up of interstellar gas, dust, and about 200 billion stars. All the stars and planets that make up the Milky Way are held together by the gravitational pull created by the mass of the galaxy.

Explain to the child that the Milky Way takes shape in the night sky as a bright cloud. This is due to the immense amount of gas and dust that are illuminated by the stars of the galaxy. This awe-inspiring sight is what gives the Milky Way its name. In fact, it was given this name by the ancient Greeks because they thought it resembled spilled milk in the sky.

If the child is a little more advanced, explain the fact that the Milky Way is constantly moving and spinning. For instance, explain that Earth is located in the outer arm of the Milky Way and takes approximately 225 million years to complete one orbit around the center of the galaxy. This rotation and movement of the galaxy can be likened to a huge spinning top with the stars and planets spinning round and round.

Next, explain to the child that although our home is the Milky Way, there are billions of other galaxies out in the universe. Explain that all of these galaxies differ in size and shape, but all of them contain stars, planets, and dust.

To summarize all the information, explain to the child that the Milky Way is a vast spiral-shaped formation of stars, planets, gas, and dust held together by gravity. It's so big that it takes us 225 million years to go around it once, and it takes up the entire night sky in many locations.

The Milky Way is an amazing and stunning entity that fascinates all who witness its many wonders, including those of ten and under.

CHAPTER ELEVEN

CAN HUMAN GO TO GALAXY

The idea of humans traveling to and living in galaxies is an exciting one. For centuries, people have looked up at the stars in the night sky and wondered if it was possible to travel between them. Although there are many obstacles standing in the way of achieving such a feat, it is certainly within the realm of possibility.

The most pressing issue that faces any potential interstellar journey is the physical limitations of our current technology. Despite the tremendous advances that have been made in propulsion technology over the past century, humanity still has not developed a form of propulsion capable of propelling an interstellar vessel through the vast distances between solar systems. This is primarily due to a simple lack of available energy. On Earth, most forms of propulsion rely on chemical reactions which are limited in terms of how fast they can propel an object. Nuclear powered propulsion is a potential candidate but it too has its drawbacks. Furthermore, even if a viable propulsion system were to be developed, it would take a significant amount of time and resources to construct a light-speed craft.

Another hurdle in the path of space exploration is the unnerving amount of hazards that lurk outside of our atmosphere. From dangerous black holes and asteroids to deadly radiation and cosmic rays, any interstellar journey would require the successful navigation of a multitude of hazards. Even if a vessel were to survive the journey to its destination, the crew members would have to be in a state of suspended animation or a form of hibernation in order to travel such vast distances in a short amount of time.

The idea of humans traveling to and living in galaxies is an exciting one, but one that could be centuries away. That said, there are still ways in which humanity can explore the other galaxies in the universe. Automated probes and robotic spacecraft can be sent to explore interstellar regions without the need for human intervention. Additionally, advances in telescope technology can enable us to observe distant galaxies and even peer out into the far reaches of the cosmos.

Although it may be a while before any human set foot in a galaxy, the prospect of interstellar travel is an exciting one that merits continued research and exploration. With continued effort, the day may come when our descendants embark on an interstellar journey and explore the wonders of the universe.

CHAPTER TWELVE

CLOSEST GALAXY TO EARTH

The Milky Way is one of the largest galaxies in the universe, but it is not the only galaxy out there. In fact, there are a multitude of galaxies in our observable universe. The closest galaxy to Earth, however, is the Andromeda Galaxy.

The Andromeda Galaxy is a barred spiral galaxy located within the Local Group of galaxies. It is the largest galaxy in the Local Group, bigger even than our own Milky Way. As such, it is an object of scientific fascination, owing to its size, its structure, and the many galaxies that orbit it.

The Andromeda Galaxy is estimated to be around 2.5 million light-years away from Earth, making it the closest galaxy to us. Its exact distance from us is difficult to ascertain due to its large size, but it is estimated to occupy an area of around 110,000 light-years across. That means it would take a beam of light 2.5 million years to traverse the distance between Earth and the Andromeda Galaxy.

The nature of the Andromeda Galaxy is one of constant motion and activity. Along with many of its satellite galaxies, the Andromeda Galaxy is involved in an ongoing galactic dance, evolving, decaying, and regenerating over time. The stars within it are constantly in motion, tracing out their orbits around the center of the galaxy. Supernovas also occur within the Andromeda Galaxy, with new ones appearing as old stars die off.

The Andromeda Galaxy also demonstrates a variety of interesting phenomena. For example, its nucleus harbors a supermassive black hole estimated to be around 400,000 solar masses in size. Recent observations have also revealed the presence of a mysterious structure known as the "Fingers of God", believed to be a cosmic filament of dark matter caused by the interactions of galaxies within the Local Group.

Given its proximity to Earth, the Andromeda Galaxy is one of the most studied galaxies in the universe. Its size, structure, and motion make it a scientific marvel, providing valuable insight into the workings of the cosmos. As such, it is likely to remain an object of interest for years to come and will no doubt continue to reveal new and exciting information about our universe.

CHAPTER THIRTEEN

HOW MANY EARTH ARE IN THE MILKY WAY

The Milky Way is our home galaxy, a vast collection of stars that stretch across the night sky. It is believed to house as many as a hundred billion stars, making it one of the largest galaxies within a radius of some 120,000 light-years. Of those stars, just one has been confirmed as a home for life—Earth.

But how many other Earths are out there hidden among the stars? This is a question that has puzzled scientists for decades and has been the subject of vigorous debate.

The truth is, we don't know exactly how many Earths might be within the Milky Way. Astronomers estimate that the chances of finding other Earth-like planets are quite high, but with so many stars and so much unknown space, it's impossible to know for certain.

However, recent discoveries have shed some light on the

matter. In the past few years, scientists have discovered thousands of planets orbiting other stars, many with Earth-like characteristics.

Based on this research, it is thought that planets similar to Earth, or at least capable of sustaining complex life, are abundant throughout the universe. Some estimates put the number at over 500 million in the Milky Way alone.

It is thought that planets similar to Earth would have certain qualities in common. Such planets would need to be in the 'habitable zone' of a star, meaning that it is at just the right distance from the star to receive moderate temperatures. Also, these planets would need to be formed out of elements similar to those found on Earth and, most importantly, a rocky surface or atmosphere capable of supporting and sustaining complex life forms.

On the other hand, there are many scientists who believe there are too many variables in the universe to accurately estimate the exact number of Earth-like planets. Others argue that many of these Earth-like planets are not even capable of sustaining life and so do not count as 'Earth', thus making it impossible to know how many true 'Earths' there are.

Ultimately, exactly how many Earths are out there remains a mystery, and the answer may remain so for many decades to come. However, what's certain is that the Milky Way is a vast and living place, one whose secrets are only just being unlocked by science. Regardless of how many Earths may exist, one thing is clear—the universe is a place of extraordinary beauty and fascinating complexity.

CHAPTER FOURTEEN

BEYOND GALAXY

What lies beyond the galaxy? That is one of the greatest mysteries of the universe and still remains largely unexplored. The universe can be understood as having millions or even billions of galaxies, each one composed of hundreds of billions of stars, separated from each other by an immense space of emptiness. But at the same time, the universe as we know it also has many so-called dark regions - tremendous regions of unknown and unseen matter. These dark regions separate galaxies from each other and separate the galaxies from the universe beyond.

What is beyond our universe? The answer is not so easily given. Some speculate that the universe is finite and limited to what we can observe, while others believe that it is infinite and may even contain whole other "universes" within it. To date, however, no one has been able to conclusively answer this question.

The truth is that we do not have enough information to make any definite statements about what lies beyond the galaxy. However, what is clear is that it likely contains some fundamental elements of the universe that have yet to be identified.

One possible source of this unknown matter could be intergalactic matter. This is the matter that lies between galaxies, which can be extremely thin gas, metal particles, and even dust. Scientists estimate that intergalactic matter makes up nearly 90% of the matter in the universe, but it has been difficult to observe due to its density and extremely low temperature. The matter contained within this dark zone could contain dark matter, which is believed to be the driving force behind much of the large-scale structure and evolution of galaxies.

Other possible sources of matter and energy beyond the galaxy include dark matter, dark energy, and possibly even another type of matter that is completely unknown to us. Dark matter is the invisible and undetectable matter that is believed to make up a large portion of the universe, yet still remains a mystery. Dark energy is the strange force that scientists believe is responsible for accelerating the expansion of the universe. Finally, some have speculated that our universe may contain another type of matter, sometimes called "strangelets", which could be the source of all matter and energy in the universe.

In conclusion, what lies beyond the galaxy is still largely unanswered. What is clear, however, is that the universe beyond our own galaxy likely contains a great deal of mystery, including dark matter, dark energy, and possibly even unknown forms of matter. Exploring this realm may shed light on some of the greatest mysteries of the universe, including the origin and the future of our universe. Only time and science can tell what lies beyond the galaxy.

CHAPTER FIFTEEN

SCIENTIFIC ANALYSIS OF MILKY WAY

The Milky Way is an immense system of stars and planets that stretches across the cosmos. It is estimated to be 100,000 light-years in diameter, and it is orbited by some 200 billion stars. In 2019, a team of scientists from the European Space Agency released a new map of the Milky Way, one of the first of its kind ever produced.

The map is highly detailed, with unprecedented accuracy and resolution. The team was able to use data from the Gaia spacecraft to measure the 3D positions of more than 1.7 billion stars, making this the most comprehensive census of stars in our galaxy yet. With this data, the team was able to create a view of the Milky Way from the inside, measuring the stellar density and its structure as a function of Galaxy radius and position.

Scientists found that the Milky Way is divided into a disk with four spiral arms and a slowly rotating bar of stars in its center called the Galactic Bar. This was confirmed in the new map, providing researchers with an exact model of the Milky Way's structure that can be used in future studies. The model also revealed that the curvature of the arms varies, indicating that the spiral structure of the Milky Way is likely more complex than previously thought.

Furthermore, the map showed the halo of stars outside the galactic plane, which was previously largely uncharted. This halo — which is thought to be a structural remnant of the Milky Way's chaotic formation —was found to be more extended than previously believed, extending to a distance of 97,000 light-years from the galactic centre.

Though this new map is just a single snapshot in time, it is a major breakthrough for astrophysics. The map marks the start of a new era in our research into the Milky Way, providing a powerful tool for uncovering the secrets of our galaxy and beyond. Ultimately, this map could help scientists gain further insight into the origin and evolution of the Milky Way and its satellite galaxies, which can help us better understand our place in the wider universe.

Contact

DR. JAGADEESH PILLAI

9839093003

myrichindia@gmail.com

facebook.com/drjagadeeshpillai

drjagadeeshpillai@youtube

www.JAGADEESHPILLAI.com

9 798889 091004

Printed by Libri Plureos GmbH in Hamburg, Germany